Queendom Tips

From A to Z

By: Tracy Manley

Copyright © 2025 Tracy Manley

All rights reserved. It is illegal to reproduce, duplicate, or transmit any part of this document electronically or in printed format. Copying this publication is strictly prohibited, and any replication of this document is not allowed unless written permission is obtained from TRACY MANLEY.

Heaven's Collective Publishing

ISBN: 979-8-218-59241-7

Dedication

To the ladies of the Queendom, thank you for being the first to take this journey with me.

Table of Contents

Introduction	p. 5	Day 15- O	p. 55
Day 1- A	p. 7	Day 16- P	p. 60
Day 2- B	p. 10	Day 17- Q	p. 64
Day 3- C	p. 13	Day 18- R	p. 68
Day 4- D	p. 16	Day 19- S	p. 72
Day 5- E	p. 19	Day 20- T	p. 75
Day 6- F	p. 22	Day 21- U	p. 78
Day 7- G	p. 26	Day 22- V	p. 81
Day 8- H	p. 29	Day 23- W	p. 84
Day 9- I	p. 33	Day 24- X	p. 87
Day 10- J	p. 36	Day 25- Y	p. 91
Day 11- K	p. 40	Day 26- Z	p. 94
Day 12- L	p. 44		
Day 13- M	p. 47		
Day 14- N	p. 51		

Introduction

This book was birthed from a challenge and a journey that I took with God and the ladies in the Queendom, which is a tribe that I lead. In the middle of the 4th quarter of 2024, God told me to pour into the women in the community. He led me to focus on encouragement, going from A to Z. Over the next 26 days, we journeyed together through 26 Queendom Tips.

We have over 1,000 members in the Queendom tribe, and we are still growing. Near the end of 2024, God challenged me to take a step out when he told me to turn the posts of the Queendoom Tips into a book, which is why you are reading this right now. I shared it with my Coach, and the journey to birth this book began.

Over the next few days, these Queendom tips hope to help women like you live a more fulfilled life. This book is designed as a devotional so that we can take a 26-day journey together. I want to challenge you to commit yourself to reading this book every day.

Let's Start with a Prayer:

Father, I thank you for your daughter reading this book right now. I pray that you speak to her and minister to her heart over the next 26 days. I pray for her courage as she journeys forward. Lord, allow her to experience transformation and step into her new.

What are you hoping to gain during this journey?

_____
_____
_____

Day 1- A
Be Adaptable

Adaptable
Able to adjust to new conditions and be modified for a new use or purpose.

There is power in your ability to be adaptable because it shows that you can be flexible when life throws curve balls. Therefore, you must learn how to be more Adaptable. We must embrace the reality that things won't remain the same forever. For example, we can't eat in our 40s what we ate in our 20s because our metabolism changes. We can't spend in our 50s what we spent in our 30s because our priorities change. We can't move in our 60s how we moved in our 40s because our body composition changes. We can't worry in our 70s about everything and everyone we did in our 50s because it will cause change to every good organ we have left. The truth is that we must adapt to what life throws at us daily as the seasons of life change.

Change can be scary, which is why many don't like to consider the importance of adaptability. We hope that things will remain the same. However, greater growth and development only come when you are willing to change the status quo. As Queens, we cannot be afraid of the inevitable changes that will come in this life; instead, we must be able to navigate change with grace by being adaptable.

Don't run away from "what ifs;" instead, consider them. This is not to insight fear but to have a strategy for maneuvering well because you have considered all the possibilities. Businesses and ministries consider all possibilities, so there are systems in place if things do not go in the direction of the original plan.

The truth is, feelings change, conditions change, pay changes, and people change, but with God, we can adapt to them all.

Philippians 4:11-12: "11 Not that I was ever in need, for I have learned how to be content with whatever I have. 12 I know how to live on almost nothing or with everything. I have learned the secret of living in every situation, whether it is with a full stomach or empty, with plenty or little."

Today, allow yourself to accept change. Pray and ask God what areas of your life you are trying to maintain control, although you should embrace change.

Day 2- B
Be Balanced

Balance
A condition in which different elements are equal or in the correct proportions.

Balance can be defined as mental and emotional steadiness, while "tilted" describes a state of emotional imbalance, typically characterized by frustration, irritation, and disappointment. If you don't gain anything else today, sis, please gain clarity and full understanding of the balancing act we've all been playing that first starts in our minds.

It's so important to fight for a well-balanced life. You can't always be Jill with the skills, Wendy with the wisdom, Princess with the plan, MoNaye with the

Money, or Rita with the ride and let everything and everybody slide. Too much of a thing isn't good, and not enough of a thing isn't good either. It can never be all work and no play. You can never give all and never receive anything in return.

Stop trying to love the heaven out of someone while loving yourself straight to hell. Stop trying to fix the world's problems while letting your problems bury you. Furthermore, stop saying YES to everything and beat yourself up because you wanted to say NO. When we operate from this place, we lose ourselves mentally, we drain every cell out of our batteries, and we walk around Tilted, Tired, Terrified, and Toxic because BALANCE is beneath us and not WITHIN US! FIX YOUR SCALES SIS, AND RECALIBRATE YOUR LIFE FROM A TO Z.

Ecclesiastes 3 NLT: A Time for Everything
3 For everything there is a season,

a time for every activity under heaven.

2 A time to be born and a time to die.

A time to plant and a time to harvest.

3 A time to kill and a time to heal.

A time to tear down and a time to build up.

4 A time to cry and a time to laugh.

A time to grieve and a time to dance.

5 A time to scatter stones and a time to gather stones.

A time to embrace and a time to turn away.

6 A time to search and a time to quit searching.

A time to keep and a time to throw away.

7 A time to tear and a time to mend.

A time to be quiet and a time to speak.

8 A time to love and a time to hate.

A time for war and a time for peace.

There is a time for so many different seasons of life. You cannot move at 100 mph every day. There are some days you have to reserve your energy and rest for the next time 100 mph is required. Make time to rest today and create a plan that includes rest in your daily or weekly routine.

Day 3- C
Be Creative

Creative
Relating to or involving the imagination or original ideas, especially in the production of an artistic work.

It's OK to color the outside of the lines and create new borders. Packing up your little box and building a bigger one is OK. Being creative involves your imagination or original ideas. This is why you must be OK and not be what others call normal. It's time to stop looking for the standard and become the Exception!

We can't raise children as our parents raised us, so we must step out of the box and set these young moms on a new course. It takes creative minds, not standing legs, to get it done. We can't make ends meet on one income all the time, so we must become creative with our skills and create a better outcome.

Whatever you do better than anyone else, find that creative ability in your makeup and use it to put some extra finances in your pocket. Some of you have one piece to the puzzle to rehab your neighborhoods, one has a piece to tackle gang initiation, and one has the piece to bring male role models to boys with no father figures. Only creatively putting all the pieces together will ignite change. Then, never be afraid to collaborate with other Queens and Kings to help get these masterpieces done.

Sis, wear the stripes and polka dots; wear what looks crazy but makes you feel beautiful. Mix the colors, add the bell bottoms, pull out the flannel, sew it, and accessorize it because the world is waiting for you to step out of the box and show them how it's done.

Unlimited ideas are waiting to come from your head onto paper and then be brought to life. Stop waiting for all the puzzle pieces to start creating the masterpiece. Use what you have until you can create everything you want. What looks crazy to some is cute and creative to others. You are the only popular opinion you need!

Ephesians 2:10: "For we are God's handiwork, created in Christ Jesus to do good works, which God prepared in advance for us to do."

Just as we are God's masterpieces, he allows us to operate in his nature to create masterpieces that will bring hope, healing, and heaven to earth. Don't deny the world of you and your creativity.

Day 4- D
Be Diligent

Diligent
Having or showing care and conscientiousness in one's work or duties.

Demonstrating diligence requires steadfastness, earnestness, and vigorous effort. Now is not the time for complacency or sluggishness; it's time to accelerate and reach our full potential. This season demands productivity, accomplishment, and substantial growth. Consistent effort yields progress in all we do.

We must become steadfast and relentless in our quest to excel by prioritizing sustainability over entertainment, rearranging our schedules to align with our goals, and earnestly evaluating our habits and surroundings to eliminate things that consistently slow us down.

Life isn't a race, but diligently pursuing a better life is crucial in maximizing what's in us and reaching our full potential. Therefore, we must be diligent in the days ahead to become the Queens we were created to be.

Don't rest until you give it your all every day for the remainder of this year. Put forth the effort now so you can afford to rest later. Put forth the effort now while you're physically able to do so. Put forth the effort now to leave a legacy for your family. Put forth the effort now so you won't fail later. Diligence requires sacrifice, but sacrifice yields good fruit in the coming days—diligence now, your heart's desires later.

Hebrews 6:11: "We want each of you to show this same diligence to the very end, so that what you hope for may be fully realized."

Proverbs 13:4: "A sluggard's appetite is never filled, but the desires of the diligent are fully satisfied."

Today, what are the areas in your life that diligence will help bring the change and transformation you truly desire? Allow yourself to prove that you can be committed, consistent, and courageous in your fulfillment of the assignment of God in your life. Your diligent efforts will not go in vain. You have the choice to be basic, good, or great. Your decision to be diligent is to be as great as God has purposed you to be.

Day 5- E
Be The Example

Example
A thing characteristic of its kind or illustrating a general rule; the standard.

As we continue this journey, I want to remind every Queen to be an example and make no excuse for it. We all have a story to tell about how we made it over. We must now become the poster child for the obstacles we overcame.

Take a moment to model your wealthy self and give another Queen tips concerning going from broke to blessed. Model your healthier self and share with a Queen how you lost 20 pounds and kept it off. Model your happy self and tell a few Queens how depression almost took you out, but God. Model your healed self (heart) and share how you learned to love yourself and how outside love became an asset, not a necessity.

Don't be modest; Don't be ashamed; and Don't worry about jealousy, envy, or whispers. The right Queen is waiting for you to be the physical example to glean from, not gossip about. I am one of those Queens sent to inspire, but I also desire to be inspired. Being an example is more than about becoming; it's also about the show and tell.

1 Timothy 4:12 New Living Translation

"12 Don't let anyone think less of you because you are young. Be an example to all believers in what you say, in the way you live, in your love, your faith, and your purity."

In the gospel, Paul tells his son, Timothy, not to allow anything to hinder him from being an example.

Today, I want to encourage you not to let anything stop you from showing up completely and fully as the light and the salt that the people around you need. Allow God to show you the way forward as a trusted example for God's purposes in the earth.

Day 6- F
Face the Facts of Forgiving

Forgive
To stop feeling angry or resentful toward someone for an offense, flaw, or mistake; cancel a debt.

We constantly hear people say forgiveness isn't for the other person but for us, and although that is very true, it is still very hard. We must start addressing or creating more steps to forgiving. There is no manual, no 10-step program, no automatic timer, and no one in the physical can rush you along. This is a journey within the soul of a human being that only God can truly help one navigate.

Today, I'm comparing forgiving to being pregnant. I know already you're wondering what this woman is talking about. In the first trimester, weeks 1 through 12, you begin to experience changes to your body that aren't visible to people but very real to you. No one can see what you're going through, and often, it requires a test to prove pregnancy and not other things. It's exciting but a little scary because it's the unknown and the period where babies are lost the most.

Forgiving someone is very similar early on. It's the unknown that causes us to slowly process forgiving those who betray us, mishandle us, cheat on us, deliberately try to sabotage us, destroy our character, or even people who just turned their backs on us. Visibly, because people can't see our pain and don't experience what we experience at the onset of the pain, they disregard the feelings they don't feel. This often leads to them creating a narrative that downplays your feelings early on.

If we are honest forgiving hurts because it means no one gets to visibly catch your wrath or experience the tables turn on them. You can't because you have to trust that God's got it. When God vindicates you, you can keep your hands and character clean. Remember that the First Trimester is critical to what you are giving birth to. Pain will always be repaid double for your trouble when you take your hands off it and your mouth.

Romans 12:19: "Dear friends, never take revenge. Leave that to the righteous anger of God. For the Scriptures say, 'I will take revenge; I will pay them back,' says the LORD."

You're giving up your right to be upset for what is more peaceful. You're giving up the wrong for the right. It's no longer your will but the will of the Father in Heaven. With God in us, we know that it's the only thing to do, but it's the scariest thing to do as well.

The early stages of forgiving mean that we must die to ourselves. We must come into agreement with peace; we must eat the Word of God daily to nourish what's growing in us; and we must pray daily to prepare for the trimesters ahead.

Matthew 6:14: "For if you forgive other people when they sin against you, your heavenly Father will also forgive you. 15 But if you do not forgive others their sins, your Father will not forgive your sins."

Today, I want you to write down a list of people you need to forgive for your own sake, purpose, and relationship with God. Unforgiveness is a poison you drink but expect others to die. Queen, we need you to live, so choose to Forgive!

Day 7- G
Grace While Growing

Grace
Undeserved favor.

We are always talking about giving Grace to others, but we seldom dig in and give Grace to ourselves. Grace is defined as an act or instance of kindness, courtesy, or compassion. We talked briefly about forgiving others, yet we often struggle more with giving ourselves the same hall pass. Today, I want to encourage you to give yourself Grace because you're still growing, Sis.

When we extend more Grace to ourselves, it builds up our self-esteem, self-worth, and self-acceptance. We begin to love the best of us more and the worst of us as we grow into a better us. There is no need to grant clemency to others and lock yourself behind bars. It's time to grab the jailer key and be set free.

Romans 8:1: "So now there is no condemnation for those who belong to Christ Jesus." You belong to Jesus Sis.

John 8:36: "So if the Son sets you free, you are truly free."

Today, you are free to let past mistakes go! Today, you are free to walk with your head held high! Today, you are free to put respect back on your name! Today, you are free to laugh at your lowest mental space!

Today, you are free to bury woulda, coulda, and shoulda and pick up The Father who created woulda,

The Son who died for Choulda, and the Holy Spirit who came to turn Shoulda into I Shall! Don't be dismayed, deterred, or destroyed by the things that Grace has already covered.

God's grace is defined as undeserved favor. Grace cannot be earned; it is something that is freely given. If God freely gives us His Grace, don't do a disservice to Him by not extending a good measure of what's been given to you. Jesus paid a price by giving you extended Grace. Don't be like most people, and don't value what you didn't have to pay for. Show value by spinning the mirror, apologizing to yourself, and accepting God's Grace.

Isaiah 30:18 NIV

"Yet the LORD longs to be gracious to you; therefore he will rise to show you compassion. For the LORD is a God of justice. Blessed are all who wait for him!"

Day 8- H
Heal at Your Own Pace

Heal
Become sound or healthy again.

We frequently hear individuals advising others to overcome their hurt and move forward. However, this is often said to be easier than actually done, and perhaps it's best left unspoken. Sometimes, people don't need your words; they just need your presence.

When you're dealing with someone who is hurting, you must be gentle and patient with the process. Sufficient emphasis is not placed on emotional healing, whereas physical recovery tends to receive more attention. Nonetheless, healing is a process that cannot be rushed, controlled, or dictated.

Proverbs 16:34: "Gracious words are a honeycomb, sweet to the soul and healing to the bones."

Healing is a process, and every process takes time. How much time it takes differs from person to person. The starting point is finding what works best for you and then taking the journey toward healing at your own pace. If you've experienced the loss of a loved one, the absence can cause you to feel a sense of hurt that's indescribable. Often, people are comforting at the onset of the loss but fail to remain consistent. I believe it's not that they don't care, but many aren't equipped to handle lasting grief. This type of healing will require you to cry out to God, seek guidance from God, lean on others who have experienced what you are going through, and possibly get therapy to make it through.

We experience divorce, loss of jobs we thought we would have forever, and loss of our faith, family, or friends. All these things require healthy healing at your pace and not the world's rat race.

What one sister needs to heal from, one sister may have easily overcome. One sister's pace doesn't dictate every sister's pace. What one sister's method was may have worked for her but not for you. Whatever you do, pace it out, or you might find yourself right back at the starting block. Here is a formula for developing your own PACE:

P- PRAY ABOUT IT

A- ACKNOWLEDGE YOUR PAIN

C- CREATE A HEALING PLAN

E- ENDURE UNTIL THE END!

Collins dictionary says if you do something at your own pace, you do it at a speed that is comfortable for you. The key factor in this definition is You—your Pace, your Race.

1 Peter 5:10: "And after you have suffered a little while, the God of all grace, who has called you to his eternal glory in Christ, will himself restore, confirm, strengthen, and establish you."

Today, I want you to be encouraged that God has given you the grace to move and heal at your pace. Allow him to grant you the liberty to go through your own process to become who he has destined you to be. This year has to be the year where you let go of the opinions of others and focus on the heart of God toward you.

Day 9- I
Identity Theft

Theft
The action or crime of stealing.

We mostly associate identity theft with fraudulent activity concerning your name, social security number, addresses, bank accounts, and credit cards, and all these are associated and important for your financial wellbeing. However, let's view it from a different angle today. The biggest identity theft taking place in the Queendom and across this nation is self-identity theft.

Self-identity is defined as the recognition of one's potential and qualities as an individual, especially in relation to social context. Sis, you have allowed the world to rob you blindly of recognizing what's in you. The very best of you was threatened the day you came out of your mother's womb. We all entered into a world of sin, and immediately, Satan was waiting to steal our identity.

Psalms 51:5: "For I was born a sinner— yes, from the moment my mother conceived me."

Some of us are still trying to bounce back from molestation at a young age... stolen purity. Some are still trying to bounce back from parental abandonment... stolen ancestry. Some are still trying to bounce back from negative word curses, a breeding ground for low self-esteem. Some of us haven't bounced back from parents who only knew what their parents taught them... leading to a lack of knowledge and sometimes causing us to be late bloomers and feeling behind the learning curve.

Whatever comes or will come to steal your identity, I want you to know that the FRAUD ALERT has been activated on your behalf today. Nothing that came to steal from you is safe from the hands of God. What came in as an imposter using your credentials will catch fire today. Your Scam protection is about to give you double for your trouble. Just repeat after me: J-E-S-U-S! Call the hotline today and get your identity back!!!

Psalms 71:20: "Though you have made me see troubles, many and bitter, you will restore my life again; from the depths of the earth, you will again bring me up. 21 You will increase my honor and comfort me once more."

Today, be excited that God is saying I am restoring what was once lost and your stolen identity and personality. Rejoice because things are about to get better because you will be better.

Day 10- J
Joy in the Journey

Joy
A feeling of great pleasure and happiness.

We arrived on day 10 of this journey. I am so proud of you for making it to this point. One of the problems that must be addressed today, which I see most often, is that many have lost their joy. True joy is what everyone needs, but it is connected to our relationship with God. Real joy means no matter what you've gone through or will go through, you are content with who you know and whose you are. You must find Joy in the Journey!

I know many have become numb to living a life full of Joy. Many truly don't believe that constant Joy is obtainable, and many believe that Joy only comes in small spurts. Mainly we believe these things because of the old saying, "If it ain't one thing, it's another," or "It's always something." It seems as though our verbiage is starting to match what we expect instead of our verbiage speaking what we are expecting as a daughter of God. We have managed to put word curses into the atmosphere and then get annoyed when we reap what we sow.

Sis, it's time to resuscitate the Joy you've always desired and speak constantly about Joy for the rest of your journey. Forgive the self-inflicted words that warded off your Joy because today, the journey to continual Joy begins. READY...SET...GO....

The Bible says in **Proverbs 18:21**: "Death and life are in the power of the tongue, And those who love it and indulge it will eat its fruit and bear the consequences of their words."

God has given us proof today that we must guard our words and thoughts to ensure that our words aren't stealing our Joy. Our words need to match where we're going, not where we've been. Our words need to produce positivity and dispel negativity. Our words must speak life over every situation seen and unseen. Our words have power, but we treat our words like batteries, almost depleted. This means we say too much without giving our words much thought, trying to get it all out as if time is escaping us too quickly. Slow down because your emotions and feelings are running a mile a minute, causing you to fly by Joy on to the next set of issues.

Today, slow down and enjoy the journey. Joy is in the journey. Therefore, it's now time to find Joy in Peace, Joy in what you love, Joy in the right people around you, Joy in alone time with you and God, Joy in the No that's really a shield of protection, Joy in sipping the coffee not chugging it down, Joy in your hobbies, and Joy knowing... OUR HOPE IS BUILT ON NOTHING LESS THAN JESUS' BLOOD AND RIGHTEOUSNESS!!!!

John 16:24: "Until now you have asked nothing in my name. Ask, and you will receive, that your joy may be full."

Proverbs 17:22: "A joyful heart is good medicine, but a crushed spirit dries up the bones."

Today, pray for your Joy to return. Ask God to help you live from a place of Joy rather than defeat hopelessness, negativity, or doubt. God is a good God, and he does have great plans for you, so live IN JOY!

Day 11- K
Kairos Moment

Kairos
Opportune moment or time.

Kairos time is referred to as the opportune time, good or proper time for action. In this sense, while Chronos is quantitative, Kairos has a qualitative, permanent nature. Plainly put, it's a God Moment in time. In the New Testament, Kairos means "the appointed time in the purpose of God," the time when God acts.

Kairos is used 86 times in the New Testament. Let's get into 22 of those times that refer to an opportune time, a "moment" or a "season" such as "harvest time."

We often hear people talk about the most precious commodity we have, that once it's gone, we can never get it back, which is time. We can't go back in time, yet we stay reminiscing on what once was. There's nothing wrong with that if you are reminiscing about a healthy place and building positively from that place. However, if you're looking back and dwelling on pain, hurt, missed opportunities, bad decisions, or missed purpose, stop now because, with God, nothing happened that He can't turn around in an instant.

You must believe YOUR KAIROS MOMENT, YOUR WIND OF GOD MOMENT, YOUR VINDICATION MOMENT, YOUR GET IT ALL BACK MOMENT, YOUR BETTER, YOUR GREATER, UNDESERVED BUT GOD GRANTED MOMENT IS HERE NOW.

Lean in and stop looking at your Chronos time which is the calendar years, days, and hours, and trust God for just one KAIROS MOMENT that can change YOUR NAME, YOUR FAMILY, YOUR SPOUSE, YOUR CHILDREN, YOUR INCOME BRACKET, YOUR ADDRESS, YOUR DESIRES, YOUR ADDICTIONS, YOUR FAITH LEVEL, YOUR TRUST AND CHANGE YOUR MOURNING INTO DANCING.

There is nothing too hard for God, and he surely will never leave or forsake you. In the Bible, Job lost everything, suffered, bled, and was left for dead, but his FAITH, TRUST, AND ENDURING LOVE FOR GOD RESTORED HIM DOUBLE FOR HIS TROUBLE.

Job 42:16: "After this, Job lived 140 years, and saw his sons and his grandsons, four generations. 17 So Job died, an old man and full of days."

Today, be encouraged that there is still time for God to show up and change everything in your life in an instance. Don't allow your current circumstances to dictate the power of the almighty God in your life.

Day 12- L
Level Up

Level
A position on a real or imaginary scale of amount, quantity, extent, or quality.

"Level Up" comes from the gaming community but has recently become the trending word for women trying to take back control of their lives. It will be very hard to level up in life until we become lovers and doers of the word of God.

This next level up will be word-verified, voice-activated, and mind-regulated. Let's Eat!

Psalms 84:11: "For the Lord God is our sun and our shield. He gives us grace and glory. The Lord will withhold no good thing from those who do what is right." Do Right and move Right on up. This Level Up will be predicated on the fruits of the spirit.

Galatians 5:22: "But the fruit of the Spirit [the result of His presence within us] is love [unselfish concern for others], joy, [inner] peace, patience [not the ability to wait, but how we act while waiting], kindness, goodness, faithfulness, 23 gentleness, self-control. Against such things, there is no law."

Simply put, leveling up means making a move for the better. When you level up using the word God, it will catapult you. God will cause you to skip steps, and God will cause you to go further faster. God will help you heal faster,

God will open up your heart to love others again; God will give you unmatched and unspeakable Joy again; and God will give you patience that will produce peace, purpose, and promise while you're waiting. God will remember your kindness and give you a just reward for it. God will continue to exchange His grace for your goodness and continued faithfulness. God extends to you His favor. For your gentleness, God will ensure that your Goliaths fall at your feet and all it requires is your Self Control.

Control your social media scroll and Level Up to God's word. Control your tongue. Level up your words to build up, not tear down. Control your thoughts and put them under subjection with the help of the Lord. Control your actions. Pray, Pause, and then Move forward. Control your environment; if it's bad soil, don't plant yourself there. Control yourself in this growing season before trying to lead others.

YOUR NEXT LEVEL WILL EITHER PRODUCE GOOD FRUIT OR BAD FRUIT. YOUR LEVEL IS PREDICATED ON THE LANE YOU CHOOSE AND THE LEVEL YOU EAT ON.

Day 13- M
Maximum Momentum

Momentum
The quantity of motion of a moving body, measured as a product of its mass and velocity.

Momentum is the powerful force that drives you toward your goals, and it's fueled by progress and positive energy. It's your driving force when moving forward and achieving your goals, and it gives you the capability to achieve more. It's true that when you begin anything, it can start slowly, but once you get started, momentum can reinforce your belief in limitless potential and possibilities.

Queen, it's Move! No matter what it looks like right now, know that you can do all things through

Christ who gives you strength (Philippians 4:13). Start using the Word to give you the power to propel forward. Rely on God's strength and not your own strength in this season. Nothing has, and nothing will be wasted.

James 1:4: "Let perseverance finish its work so that you may be mature and complete, not lacking anything."

Perseverance means continuing to do or achieve something, even when it seems difficult or may take a long time. Simply put, don't quit, but keep going, keep striving, keep putting one foot in front of the other, and keep showing up.

Stay the course and watch your spark turn to a flicker, your flicker turn into a flame, and your flame turn into a wildfire and set the rest of your life Ablaze. That's what MOMENTUM looks like.

Sis, keep building the business; keep writing the book; keep baking out of your kitchen; keep promoting your product; keep selling the product out of your car; and keep experimenting with the idea, whatever it is. Let today be the day you change your mindset. Work on it or work at it until it builds momentum and prepares you for the moment that your efforts take flight.

Queen, you've taxied the runway long enough. An airplane never gets on the runway without the intention to take off. It waits its turn, and on command, it barrels down the runway, gaining the right speed and momentum needed to thrust upward into the air. It soars to unimaginable heights until it reaches its cruising altitude and doesn't land until it reaches its destination. You're next in line, Queen, and you've been cleared for takeoff. Get in position, shake off stagnation, shoot for the stars, challenge your own complacency, tell fear about your faith, and barrel down the runway to your destiny. We've made it to M, and I know by now you're Motivated to Move with the MOMENTUM to do so.

Day 14- N
No

No
Used to give a negative response.

A solid "no" can save you time, money, energy, and additional prescription costs. No is one of the shortest yet most powerful words that many under-utilize. Often, we feel guilty when we tell someone No. Guilt comes up when saying no because you feel that you're being selfish or because you believe that you're going to hurt someone's feelings while neglecting your own feelings. That's why we often say Yes, even when we truly mean No.

It's not because you're easily persuaded, often misled, or stupid. This is usually due to a heart that's full of love, full of compassion, and full of good. The person who often says Yes because they don't want others to feel what they've felt in past seasons where rejection may have been present. The downside to this comes from those who abuse, misuse, take advantage of, or manipulate the intentions and will of those who say Yes but mean No. Some of you are strong enough to say No, throw your head back and twist off, but so many are not. So, this is for you today.

Romans 13:8: "Owe nothing to anyone except to love and seek the best for one another; for he who [unselfishly] loves his neighbor has fulfilled the [essence of the] law [relating to one's fellowman]."

Often, we don't consider that even God doesn't always give us a Yes, and He loves us. Remember John 3:16: "For God so loved the world that he gave his one

Queendom Tips

and only Son, that whoever believes in him shall not perish but have eternal life." It's time to get to the root of the problem and live free in OUR NO GIRL NO ERA. It can be difficult, but it can be done.

This is how it can be addressed: SET HEALTHY BOUNDARIES; KILL PEOPLE PLEASING BY IDENTIFYING YOUR ISSUE AND GETTING HELP WITH IT; KNOW YOUR LIMITS; DON'T BE SO QUICK TO RESPOND TO REQUEST; AND REMEMBER YOU CAN'T CORRECT OTHERS POOR CHOICES.

It can be tempting to say "yes" simply because we're afraid of disappointing someone or coming across as rude or mean. But when we say yes unwillingly, we are dishonest to ourselves and to the other person.

James 5:12: "Let your 'yes' be yes and your 'no' be no."

Today, write out reasons why you have said yes in the past. Then, pray about God helping you to say no when you should.

Day 15- O Overthinking

Overthinking
Think about something too much or for too long.

Have you ever been overwhelmed by overthinking? It is one of the greatest distractions and hindrances to purpose. What a perfect day to break the chains of OVERTHINKING off our minds and move freely into a fruitful and not fruitless weekend. We spend so much time in our own thoughts, which can seem to run amuck because we are unable to properly put the right actions into our thoughts. Instead of putting our best foot forward, we keep adding more thoughts to the original thought, ultimately causing a mental train wreck in our own minds.

We know once a train goes off track, it takes strategic planning, heavy equipment, and a good team to clean up the mess. We are no different! It takes a team: a good coach, honest family and friends, and a mind to see our issue and accept help getting right side up again. We literally could create our own reality shows, and we all know the mass ball of confusion those shows become. Season 53...Episode 11 Tracy's Mind Gone Wild. It sounds funny, but it's reality.

I know we all face this issue more than we care to admit. We create false narratives every week because we take one word and run with it. We can get a compliment and ponder it so much that it goes from a compliment to criticism.

It went from a kind gesture to "I wonder what that was all about." And just like that, the overthinking has taken over something that should have been a one-and-done.

Overthinking causes us to talk ourselves out of a blessing, flip it around, and call it a lesson. The more seasoned Saints used to say you must call a spade a spade. Queen, it's time to be your own Ace in the hole. We have chased good people away; we have run off good help; we have talked ourselves out of healthy relationships; we have buried what was sent to help us bloom; we have talked ourselves out of trusted places; we have run the right mate off; and we have drained our family out all due to overthinking. You've played this game long enough, and it's time for you to rise out of the ashes of your own mindset.

Overthinkers can get trapped in a cycle of worry and doubt, which can lead to heightened anxiety, stress, and even depression. We must get off the path of destruction and get on the progression path. We can't afford to waste another day in dysfunction, and we can't be our own natural disaster anymore. WE MUST THINK ON A HIGHER, LIVE WITH PURPOSE ON PURPOSE, TURN NEGATIVE THOUGHTS INTO POSITIVE POSSIBILITIES, SEE ON A HIGHER LEVEL, AND BECOME THE YOU THAT'S A LESSON TO OTHERS.

Proverbs 3:5-6: "Trust in the Lord with all your heart and lean not on your own understanding; in all your ways submit to him, and he will make your paths straight."

1 Peter 5:7: "Cast all your anxiety on him because he cares for you."

Philippians 4:6-7: "6 Do not be anxious about anything, but in every situation, by prayer and petition, with thanksgiving, present your requests to God.

7 And the peace of God, which transcends all understanding, will guard your hearts and your minds in Christ Jesus."

Today, identify the areas and situations you tend to overthink in your life. What should you do instead of overthinking? What will be your action plan to pull yourself out of that habit?

Day 16- P
Pursue it until you Subdue

Subdue
Overcome, quieten, or bring under control.

Pursue, according to the Urban Dictionary, means to push yourself to do something until you've attained it, and pursue could also mean to chase something or someone but for a good reason. It's not the time to give up or throw in the towel, even if you're a Cowboys fan. It's time to stand firm on the word of God, the will of God, the strength of God, the Grace of God, and go after the Promises of God.

In I Samuel 30, The Amalekites thinking they had outsmarted David came and wrecked David's camp while He and his army were away. They came and stole all of their valuables, their wives, children, and livestock and fled. Therefore, David's army came back to nothing. The men even talked about stoning David. It's interesting to see people love you in good times but plot to kill you in the sight of trouble. Nevertheless, David consulted with the Lord, and this was the response:

1 Samuel 30:8 NKJV: "So David inquired of the Lord, saying, 'Shall I pursue this troop Shall I overtake them.' And He answered him, 'Pursue, for you shall surely overtake them and without fail recover all.'"

David did as the Lord instructed. Some of the men were too weary to pursue until the end, but David used who he had left to reclaim what had been stolen from him. Ultimately, David recovered everything. The lesson of the day is....

First, the devil will come to steal your Joy, Peace, Hope, Money, and Honey, but you can't waddle or wade in the water too long. You must get up and intentionally pursue what has been stolen from you. You must want it all back. David didn't recover some; he recovered it all. We serve a God that when we ask for what's rightfully ours, He will ensure victory in the pursuit.

Second, if you trust in the Lord, you will not fail even if others around you find fault in you. While you are out pursuing, many will follow and trust you while you are winning but then waver when it looks like you are losing. Don't get caught up in the chatter; instead, lean in closer to hear the voice of God for yourself, pray earnestly until the mountains start moving, rely on God, not your natural responses, and trust God with the answer key to your test. When He says Pursue, do it without Pause.

Third, if God said it, you better believe it. Google is good, but it's not the Bible. Friends are good, but they become weary. Family is close, but they aren't always right. No matter what you've lost, put your War clothes on and go to the enemy's camp to get your stuff back.

Get your tactical gear in order.... GET YOUR PRAYER LIFE IN CHECK SO YOU CAN PURSUE WITH CONFIDENCE. GET YOUR WORD LIFE IN CHECK SO YOU CAN PURSUE WITH WISDOM. GET YOUR WORSHIP LIFE IN CHECK SO YOU CAN PURSUE WITH CLARITY. GET YOUR TIME ALONE WITH GOD IN CHECK SO YOU CAN PURSUE AND KNOW YOU HEARD FROM GOD. PURSUE IT UNTIL YOU SUBDUE IT!

Day 17- Q
Next in Queue

Queue
A line or sequence of people or vehicles awaiting their turn to be attended to or to proceed.

In life, waiting in line is not uncommon. We waited in grocery lines before self-checkout and in department store lines before Amazon and Shein took over. We waited in those super long DMV lines before we could get decals for multiple years. So, we fully know what being in QUEUE looks and feels like.

The British definition of QUEUE is a line or sequence of people awaiting their turn to be attended to or to proceed. Most of us hate waiting, but sometimes there is a blessing in the waiting.

Jeremiah 29:11: "For I know the plans I have for you, declares the LORD, plans for welfare and not for evil, to give you a future and a hope."

The beginning of a thing won't look like the ending of a thing, but you help determine the outcome of a thing. Sometimes your next is predicated on how you stand while waiting. I remember being in the lunch line in elementary school, where we had to stand in a straight line and be quiet until we went through the line and received our trays. We would often be put to the back of the line if we were disorderly. Instead of being 1st, 5th, or 8th in QUEUE, we could end up 17th in QUEUE. We all had a common interest; we were all hungry, but our obedience or lack of it could be the deciding factor on when we ate. We couldn't blame anyone but ourselves if the wait was extended because we were sent to the back of the line. This may seem simple, but our failure to wait in the right posture is exactly what we look like now failing to wait in the right posture as daughters of God.

GOD WANTS TO PUT US NEXT IN QUEUE, BUT WE CAN'T STAND STILL LONG ENOUGH TO RECEIVE OUR PORTION. WE GO OFF DOING EVERYTHING UNDER THE SUN BUT WANT GOD TO HOLD OUR POSITION IN QUEUE. WE REALLY WANT GOD TO TURN HIS HEAD TO OUR DISOBEDIENCE SO WE CAN LEAVE THE QUEUE AND THEN COME BACK AND CUT IN FRONT OF THOSE WHO HAVE OBEYED, STAYED, PRAYED, AND LAID OUT THEIR LIVES TO HAVE NEXT. WE WANT IT OUR WAY AS IF GOD IS LIKE BURGER KING... OH HE IS THE KING, BUT HIS CROWN IS THE REAL DEAL.

We repeatedly get out of QUEUE, going after things that won't satisfy us, only to return to the real thing and have to wait in QUEUE all over again. Stop jumping in and out of QUEUE so you can finally get what's been promised to you. Stop getting out of QUEUE going after every Oasis and drink from the well that never runs dry. Stop getting out of QUEUE to eat the fat of the land when the good of the land is right before you. The length of time in QUEUE varies, but the reward is worth the wait.

Job 8:7 (NASB): "Though your beginning was insignificant, yet your end will increase greatly."

Today, what are the things that have pulled you out of line in the past? What areas would have been different if you had only responded the way God has purposed for you to? What does it look like to remain in queue in this season of your life?

Day 18- R
Risky Business

Risky
Full of the possibility of danger, failure, or loss.

It's long but good today. Old school slang said, "If you're scared, say you're scared" or "scared money don't make no money." Honestly, they both had negative connotations, but they evoked an urgency in you to make a move. That move didn't seem like much then, but most of the time, it required you to take some risk, hope for a good outcome, and move from Fear to Faith.

Reverso dictionary defines risky business as a situation with uncertain outcomes. If we are honest with ourselves, we've all entered into things unsure, uncertain, and with little understanding. We've entered into partnerships, relationships, and business deals that looked funny from afar and were as shady as a palm tree in the night desert. We still took the Risk, and it was mainly blind faith, or we felt as though we could handle the Risk.

We've all engaged in a form of RISKY BUSINESS, and I bet it's because we made a decision to be strong, courageous, and trust God with the outcome.

Let's look at Ruth but keep the courage of Joshua. First, Ruth the Moabite made a move, leaving with Naomi to go to a land that she knew nothing about, to serve a God she knew nothing about, and not even knowing if she'd be accepted. Ruth was a Moabite, and I'm sure she had some differences. When she married Naomi's son, she married her customs and embraced her people.

Later, Ruth makes a RISKY decision after the death of her husband to go with her mother in love. Clearly, love, trust, and mutual respect were going on here. I even imagine Ruth may have been a little taller than the average woman. After all, we are very familiar with one of her famous fellow Moabites named Goliath. Yeah, the one David was courageous enough to fight with a slingshot and a smooth stone. Now, that's surely another example of RISKY BUSINESS.

Ruth 1:16: "But Ruth replied, 'Don't urge me to leave you or to turn back from you. Where you go, I will go, and where you stay, I will stay. Your people will be my people and your God my God.'"

Ruth took the Risk, got to Naomi's land, worked in the fields, allowed Naomi to groom her, and got Boaz's attention. Salmon was the father of Boaz (whose mother was Rahab). Boaz was the father of Obed (whose mother was Ruth). Obed was the father of Jesse. Jesse was the father of King David. Verse 16 Jacob was the father of Joseph, the husband of Mary. Mary gave birth to Jesus, who is called the Messiah.

LINEAGE DOESN'T LIE, AND RISKY BUSINESS CAN GET YOU A KING OR THE LIFE OF A KING. JUST MAKE SURE YOU'RE DOING BUSINESS WITH JESUS.

Today, consider the areas that you have been walking in more cautiously rather than operating in faith by making risky decisions with God. Why are you avoiding the risk? How can you move forward in bold faith to take risks with God?

Day 19- S
Be Steadfast

Steadfast
Resolutely or dutifully, firm, and unwavering.

When we add being steadfast to intention, we have the recipe for success in whatever our hearts and minds desire. We miss out on so many wonderful things because we move our feet too fast. We often struggle with devoting ourselves to anything or anyone. We tend to move out of emotion and obligation rather than loyalty when we start something.

To those in relationships or marriages, sometimes we have to be repaired from the inside out. He might be 6'2 and into you, but he never got the play-by-play on how to treat you, keep you, build with you, or properly love you. We must start loving one another enough to repair the breech and not sugarcoat it. Change doesn't happen overnight, but you can begin to make a change overnight. It's not too late, but it will require hard work. You must be unwavering and immovable in your quest to love and be loved.

WE'VE BEEN LOYAL AND DEVOTED TO BROKEN PEOPLE, LOYAL TO UNSTABLE PLACES, LOYAL TO BELIEF SYSTEMS ABSENT OF GOD, AND LOYAL TO CAUSES THAT DON'T CONCERN US FOR FAR TOO LONG. IT'S TIME TO CORRECT WHAT'S BEEN CRUSHING US. SOMETIMES WE NEEDED THE CRUSHING TO GET OUT OF COMPLACENCY AND COMPROMISE.

I'm not suggesting that you ever overstay your welcome or die in the desert, but if God is in it, stay long enough to win in it.

James 1:12: "Blessed is the man who remains steadfast under trial, for when he has stood the test he will receive the crown of life, which God has promised to those who love him."

Let's take it slowly and steadily, not changing our minds but charting a new course if we're already too deep. If counseling is needed to Cruise back into a healthy relationship, it's not a Curse word; it's a Cure. If you've Drifted away from God, take a Discipleship class and divert back to the shores where there is safety in His will.

Today, choose what you should remain steadfast in for the remainder of this year. This builds discipline, diligence, and determination to see the completion of an assignment.

Day 20- T
You are Tailor-Made

Tailor-made
Specially designed for a particular person or purpose.

You are tailor-made: original design, authentic, one-of-a-kind, a perfect fit, of the highest quality, and a statement piece formed and created masterfully by God. You should feel comfortable commanding attention when you enter a room because you were designed to do so.

Psalm 139:14: "I will give thanks and praise to You, for I am fearfully and wonderfully made; Wonderful are Your works, And my soul knows it very well."

We are all familiar with this passage of scripture, but we seldom HONOR IT or embrace its reality. The word "fearfully" in Hebrew can mean "with great reverence," "heartfelt interest," or "respect." The meaning of the word alone should get your attention, Queen. God took the time to Carefully Craft what He Created into a Classic. Tailor-made designs walk in authority. Tailor-made designs are given Respect when we take the Responsibility of Respecting and Representing God's brand well.

The word "wonderfully" in Hebrew can mean "unique" or "set apart." God created a Unique being not to be Underestimated, Undermined, Unused, or made to feel Unworthy. You were set apart to flourish in Desolate places, flourish in Dry places, flourish in times of Disaster, and flourish even in the valley of Dry bones. What makes you unique is the fact that you've lived through what most people would Die through.

Ephesians 2:10: "For we are God's handiwork, created in Christ Jesus to do good works, which God prepared in advance for us to do."

We don't buy expensive clothes to sit in a closet and waste away, and God didn't tailor-make us to go hide under a rock. WE MUST EMBRACE WHAT NO MAN CAN ERASE; WE MUST OWN OUR ORIGINALITY; WE MUST HIT THE RUNWAY READY EVERY DAY; WE MUST SHINE EVEN IN A STORM; AND WE MUST SQUARE OUR SHOULDERS BACK BECAUSE WE LACK NOTHING.

YOU'RE A PART OF GOD'S BRAND NOW, AND YOU CAN BOAST ABOUT BEING TAILOR-MADE BY THE MASTER DESIGNER.

Today, celebrate how God made you. Write out your strengths, skills, abilities, and positive personality traits.

Day 21- U
Unity

Unity
The state of being united or joined as a whole.

Unity can be defined as the state of being united or joined as a whole. Everyone wants their slice of the pie in this world. Sadly, many people either want the whole pie or the majority of the pie. Typically, you can get eight slices out of a pie, but some take a quarter each, leaving none for anyone else. You may laugh and think it's just pie, but truthfully, it's a recipe for a lack of Growth, Unhealthy Relationships, No Long-term Sustainability, and more.

Romans 12:16: "Live in harmony with one another. Do not be haughty, but associate with the lowly. Never be wise in your own sight."

I remember my happiest childhood moments living in a small community called Norristown. My grandmother raised her children there, and a few of her grands were born there as well. It wasn't much, but we were together, we loved, we laughed, and we gathered. Our neighbors weren't friends; they were family, and we created lifetime bonds.

Psalms 133:1: "A Song of Ascents. Of David. Behold, how good and pleasant it is when brothers dwell in unity!"

If you're in a better situation, help someone who may not be. SHARE THE PIE. If you figured out a better way to support your family, SHARE THE PIE. If you made it out of abuse, don't watch others suffer alone; SHARE THE PIE. If you overcame addiction, SHARE THE PIE.

DON'T JUST SAY WE ARE BETTER TOGETHER; LIVE LIFE LIKE WE ARE BETTER TOGETHER, MOVE LIKE WE ARE BETTER TOGETHER, GIVE LIKE WE ARE BETTER TOGETHER, EDUCATE LIKE WE ARE BETTER TOGETHER, AND LOVE LIKE WE ARE BETTER TOGETHER BECAUSE THERE IS NO SUCCESSFUL COMMUNITY WITHOUT UNITY.

1 Peter 3:8: "Finally, all of you, have unity of mind, sympathy, brotherly love, a tender heart, and a humble mind."

Day 22- V
Victory

Victory
An act of defeating an enemy or opponent in a battle, game, or other competition.

Your name is VICTORY!

V...View battles differently

I...Insured the Win

C...Courageous in battle

T...Trained to recover all

O...Overcome every Obstacle

R...Rise to every occasion

Y...Your name is Vicory

1 Corinthians 15:57: "but thanks be to God, who gives us the victory [as conquerors] through our Lord Jesus."

Believe in the word of God, and be confident in believing in the Word working for you. You're more than a CONQUEROR, AND EVEN IF YOU HAVE TO CRY, CRAWL, OR CREEP TO THE FINISH LINE, VICTORY AWAITS YOU. THE BATTLE IS WON AND EVERYONE IS WAITING FOR YOU TO CLAIM YOUR PRIZE.

Deuteronomy 20:4: "For the Lord your God is he who goes with you to fight for you against your enemies, to give you the victory."

You're never fighting alone. Never throw up the white flag in defeat, never surrender to a challenge, face it head-on, never retreat from the battle, instead put on the full armor of God, and NEVER QUIT BEFORE YOU EVEN GET STARTED.

Today, laugh because you LACK NOTHING. Laugh because even the last LOST WAS ONLY TRAINING FOR THE NEXT DECADE OF WINS. Laugh because the enemy tried it, but you shall TRIUMPH OVER EVERY TACTIC. Laugh because the enemy only came to throw curve balls your way only to realize that you abide under the shadow of the almighty and you dwell.

Day 23- W
It is Well

Well
In a good or satisfactory way; in a thorough manner.

Today, we will get a Queendom history lesson. IT IS WELL. I think I have leaned on these three words so much in 2024 that they have become my natural response to any situation.

"IT IS WELL" is a classic song that most of us have heard. The condensed message is finding peace in the midst of suffering. It is a testament to the power of faith and the resilience of the human spirit. We've gone through so much, seen so much, heard so much, and conditioned ourselves to say IT IS WELL.

The song's lyric writer, Horatio Spafford, knew something about life's unexpected challenges. He was a successful attorney and real estate investor who lost a fortune in the great Chicago fire of 1871. Around the same time, his four-year-old son died of scarlet fever. His story doesn't end there. Two years later, on a voyage to Europe, his wife and daughters were on a ship that was hit mid-voyage. His wife was saved, but his four daughters died. Whew, these lyrics make even more sense to me now:

"When peace like a river attendeth my way,

when sorrows like sea billows roll;

whatever my lot, Thou hast taught me to say,

"It is well, it is well with my soul.""

PERHAPS THE SONG WAS BIRTH OUT OF PAIN. BUT IT'S HIS FAITH THAT RESONATES WITH ME MORE THAN HIS PAIN. Losing my Aunt last week was hard, but I know you make no mistakes even when death makes no sense- IT IS WELL. Many of you going through holiday seasons can be emotionally bankrupt, but you have to muster up the strength- IT IS WELL. It doesn't remove our hurt or pain but allows our HOLY GOD TO SEE OUR HEARTS CRY!

Psalm 46:1-3: "God is our refuge and strength, a very present help in trouble. Therefore will not we fear, though the earth be removed, and though the mountains be carried into the midst of the sea; Though the waters thereof roar and be troubled, though the mountains shake with the swelling thereof."

Today, what do you need to take victory in? Allow yourself to realize that the enemy is trying to take away your sense of victory when Jesus has made us victorious through his death, burial, and resurrection. Pray boldly about the situation that has been getting the best of you.

Day 24- X
X-ray

X-ray
An electromagnetic wave of high energy and very short wavelength, which is able to pass through many materials opaque to light.

When we think of an X-ray, we normally think of it in a medical sense. It's not an everyday occurrence in our lives, but it must be done when there is a need. The naked eye can't see what an X-Ray can see. X-rays are commonly used to look at bones and joints to diagnose other conditions quickly. We see the importance of a physical X-ray, but now let's dig into my God-inspired importance of Him being our spiritual X-ray machine.

It would be amazing if we could just pull out a pocket X-ray machine and do a full head scan on people that would reveal their thoughts and intentions immediately. UNFORTUNATELY, WE ARE LEFT TO BELIEVE WHAT PEOPLE SAY UNTIL THEY SHOW US DIFFERENTLY.

Most of us are tired of trying to figure people out, so we just stay docked or jump ship when building relationships. We exit the Zones of Friendship, Relationship, Churchship, Socialship, Loveship, and ultimately Godship because we can only view things at SEE (SEA) level. Yeah, a few made-up words, but you get the gist.

1 Samuel 16:7: "But the Lord said to Samuel, 'Don't judge by his appearance or height, for I have rejected him. The Lord doesn't see things the way you see them. People judge by outward appearance, but the Lord looks at the heart.'"

When Samuel went to anoint the next king, he was using the naked eye. He was picking a King based on physical appearance. Much like some of us, we picked what we were physically attracted to, not knowing that what we see can't always determine what we are going to get. Our vision can be so cloudy that we miss steps and rush the exams; we use the instant, sometimes unreliable testing methods and get what we were looking at, but often, it's not what we asked for. STOP GETTING CAUGHT AT SEE LEVEL. GET TO THE HEART LEVEL. IT TAKES MORE TIME, BUT YOU END UP WITH LESS TROUBLE.

We don't have a pocket X-ray machine, but we do have God our Father, who loved us enough to send Jesus his Son to die on a rugged cross and ascend back to heaven. Jesus now sits on the right side of God, constantly interceding for us. Then, the Holy Spirit fully acts as our helper and guide if we allow him.

Therefore, we have an X-ray machine; we just have to stay plugged in to it.

Just like an X-ray machine needs power to be activated, we must stay powered up. WE NEED TO STAY IN THE POSTURE OF PRAYER; WE NEED TO WORSHIP WHILE WAITING ON GOD TO REVEAL THE TRUTH; WE NEED TO USE GODLY DISCERNMENT, NOT WORLDLY INTUITION, BECAUSE GOD SPEAKS CONCERNING WHAT WE CAN'T SEE; AND LASTLY, WE NEED TO RIGHTFULLY DIVIDE THE WORD OF GOD BECAUSE IN IT WE WILL FIND ALL THE TRUTH.

Today, what areas of your life do you need to allow the X-ray machine of the Holy Spirit to be activated so you can regain your peace, joy, and strength for the next season?

Day 25- Y
Let Your Yes by Your Yes

Yes
Used to give an affirmative response.

I've realized that a solid Yes can be as difficult as a solid No. Until recently, I was that Yes girl. I wasn't saying Yes out of a pleasing place; I was saying Yes out of a needed place.

If you've ever dealt with rejection, loss, isolation, or absence of a parent, it tends to weigh heavily on how you treat others. Be careful; people can smell your needs from miles away. Some become over-extenders, while others become overprotective of themselves. SOME YESES ARE TO FULFILL A NEED, NOT NECESSARILY TO PLEASE.

Let this year be taking back our solid Yes from the wrong places and Standing on Business with that shaky Yes to God. Some of you need to pack up your strong Yes in an area and apply that Yes to an area that serves you better. If you give a strong Yes to anything, lean in Queen... make sure it benefits you, brings you joy, makes you smile, loves you in and out of your face, speaks well of you, or pushes you to destiny.

Matthew 5:37: "But let your 'Yes' be 'Yes,' and your 'No,' 'No.' For whatever is more than these is from the evil one."

Can I just encourage you at this moment? Before you truly give Man a Yes, please give God a Yes first. You will need God to help you make sound decisions and judge well, and, for lack of better words, God can help you pick right. Sometimes, you have to sit in your own choices and see where you didn't Confer with or Choose God's way.

Today, you can choose to reinforce your Yes with God, your spouse, your children, your business, your bff, yourself, or a situation. READY SET GO. Also, ensure it's done from the right place, for the right reason, and in the right season.

1 Corinthians 16:14: "And do everything with love."

Day 26- Z
Zeal to Seal the Deal

Zeal
Great energy or enthusiasm in pursuit of a cause or an objective.

We have now reached the pinnacle, marked by the letter Z, which serves as a perfect ending. Zeal, as per its definition, embodies the great energy or enthusiasm directed towards a cause or objective. Thanks to your encouragement, patience, and exemplary zeal, we are well-equipped to set, initiate, and fulfill our goals.

I've spent 26 days unsure of how the Queendom would respond to longer posts, but I was determined to exemplify a strong commitment to God, myself, and all of you. I'm out of the starting blocks now, and it's no looking back. THIS IS FINISHED, BUT I'M STILL IN THE BIRTHING POSITION.

Joshua 1:2-5: 2 "Moses my servant is dead. Therefore, the time has come for you to lead these people, the Israelites, across the Jordan River into the land I am giving them. 3 I promise you what I promised Moses: 'Wherever you set foot, you will be on land I have given you— 4 from the Negev wilderness in the south to the Lebanon mountains in the north, from the Euphrates River in the east to the Mediterranean Sea in the west, including all the land of the Hittites.' 5 No one will be able to stand against you as long as you live. For I will be with you as I was with Moses. I will not fail you or abandon you."

I'm reminding you just as God reminded Joshua to be STRONG AND COURAGEOUS as you engage this year. DON'T START WEAK AND WEARY; START

STRONG and FINISH STRONG. We are all called to work in our HOMES, CHURCH, JOBS, BUSINESS, SOCIAL ORGANIZATIONS, SCHOOLS, COMMUNITY, AND EVEN IN OURSELVES. It's your time to get Excited, Enthusiastic, and Energetic and Execute Every Endeavor with Excellence and Even more Zeal.

YOU'RE OUT HERE NOW; YOU'VE BEEN EQUIPPED FROM A TO Z. I'VE PROVEN WHAT CAN BE DONE WHEN ACTION AND GOD IDEAS COLLIDE. THE SCRIPTURE TELLS YOU TODAY THAT GOD IS WITH YOU.

Get your flowers now, Queens, while you can smell and enjoy their beauty. Go forth and be a finisher because the ANOINTING is on you!

YOUR ZEAL WILL SEAL THE DEAL!

About the Author

Tracy C. Manley is a dynamic and inspiring figure who seamlessly embodies the roles of a wife, mother, daughter, spiritual life coach, and entrepreneur. Residing in the charming small town of Waverly, Virginia, Tracy is deeply rooted in her community and dedicated to positively impacting the lives of those around her. She knows firsthand the challenges of balancing family, life's demands, and a thriving career, which fuels her passion for motivating and empowering women to pursue their dreams despite any obstacles or setbacks they may encounter.

Through engaging writing and transformative coaching, Tracy has become a beacon of hope and encouragement for countless women seeking to overcome life's hurdles. She is a committed servant of the Lord and a staunch advocate for the principles of

Unity, Love, and Service. These foundational beliefs guide her actions and inspire her efforts as she works tirelessly to uplift those in need.

As the Founder of The Conquering Queen, Tracy has created a powerful platform designed to strengthen, encourage, empower, and catapult women into their God-given destinies. She believes that every woman possesses the potential to achieve greatness, and she dedicates her time to helping them recognize and harness that inner strength. Tracy's unwavering commitment to her mission is evident in her hands-on approach to community service, whether organizing events, leading workshops, or simply lending a helping hand, and she is always on the front lines.

Tracy's personal life is a testament to her dedication and resilience. Married to her husband, Andre Manley, they share a blended family of five wonderful children: Jaquan, Najae, Andrea, India, and

Jada. This family dynamic enriches Tracy's life, giving her a unique perspective on the importance of love, support, and understanding within the family unit. Tracy and Andre also co-own Manley Maid Inc., combining their entrepreneurial spirit with a shared vision of success.

Her faith plays a pivotal role in everything she does. Tracy's favorite scripture, Luke 22:31-32, serves as a reminder of the power of prayer and the importance of perseverance: "Simon, Simon, Satan has asked to sift all of you as wheat. But I have prayed for you, Simon, that your faith may not fail. And when you have turned back, strengthen your brothers." These words resonate deeply with Tracy, reinforcing her belief that no matter the challenges, she is equipped with the strength and support to navigate them and uplift others.

Tracy C. Manley exemplifies what it means to be a true leader and servant in every aspect of her life. Her energetic spirit, commitment to God and community, and relentless pursuit of excellence inspire those around her to strive for their own victories. With a heart full of compassion and a mind focused on empowerment, Tracy continues to break barriers and pave the way for women everywhere to step boldly into their destinies.

www.ingramcontent.com/pod-product-compliance
Lightning Source LLC
Chambersburg PA
CBHW032008080426
42735CB00007B/544